WE'RE ALL IN THIS TOGETHER
HOW FAMILIES MATTER

DISCARDED

Titles in This Set

Cover Artist

Randall Enos combines linoleum-cut prints and
collage in his work—a technique that he invented
himself. When he is not busy making his very special
prints for newspapers, magazines, and books such as
this one, you might find him spending time with his
pet gopher snake, a member of the Enos household
for over twenty-five years.

ISBN: 0-673-80043-1

Acknowledgments appear on page 128.

345678910RRS999897969594 93

WE'RE ALL IN THIS TOGETHER

HOW FAMILIES MATTER

ScottForesman

A Division of HarperCollinsPublishers

CONTENTS

Children Write About Families
Genre Study

Eloise Greenfield Writes About Families
Author Study

Student Resources

NO ONE IS GOING TO NASHVILLE

—— by Mavis Jukes ——
illustrations by Lloyd Bloom

It was six o'clock in the morning.

Sonia checked her alligator lizard. He was out of termites, and possibly in a bad mood. She decided to leave him alone. Nobody else was up except Ms. Mackey, the goose. She was standing on the back deck, talking to herself.

Sonia sat in the kitchen with her knees inside her nightgown. She peered out the window. The moon was still up above the rooftops. The houses were beginning to pale.

There was a dog on the stoop! He was eating radishes on the mat.

Sonia opened the door. "Hello doggy!" she said. She knelt down. "You like radishes?"

He licked her face.

"Have you been into the garbage?"

He signaled to her with his ears.

"Stay!" said Sonia. She went back in the house and clattered in the pot cupboard.

"What time is it, Sonia?" her father called from the bedroom.

Sonia didn't answer because he had forgotten to call her "Dr. Ackley." She filled the bottom of the egg poacher with water and left it on the stoop, then went into the house and to the bedroom. "Dad," she said. "What do you think is a good name for a dog?"

He was trying to doze. "I'm closing my eyes and thinking," he lied.

Sonia waited. "You're sleeping!" she said.

He opened one eye. "Names for dogs. Let's see. Dog names. Ask Annette. She's the dog lover. What *time* is it?"

"About six fifteen," said Annette. "I heard the train go by a few minutes ago." She rolled over.

Sonia went over to her stepmother's side of the bed. "Annette!" she said. "What name do you like for a dog?"

Annette propped herself up on her elbows. Her hair fell onto the sheets in beautiful reddish loops. "A dog name? My favorite? Maxine. Absolutely. I used to have a dog named Maxine. She ate cabbages." Annette collapsed on the pillow.

"Here, Maxine!" called Sonia.

"Oh no," said her father. He slid beneath the blankets. "I can't stand it! Not a dog at six o'clock in the morning!"

The dog padded through the door and into the bedroom.

"Maxine," said Sonia, "I want you to meet my father, Richard, and my Wicked Stepmother, Annette."

Annette got up. "That's not a Maxine," she reported, "that's a Max." She put on Richard's loafers and shuffled into the kitchen.

Richard got up and put on his pants. Sonia and Max watched him search for his shoes. Max's ears were moving so wildly they could have been conducting a symphony.

"Weird ears," said Richard. He went into the kitchen.

Ms. Mackey stared through the glass at his feet and started honking. He opened the door a couple of inches. *"Quiet!"* he whispered. "You're not even supposed to live inside the city limits!"

She puffed her feathers.

"Beat it!" said Richard. "Go eat some snails!"

Off she waddled.

Sonia came into the kitchen wearing white pants and a white shirt with DR. S. ACKLEY, D.V.M. printed on the pocket with a felt-tip pen. She took something from the refrigerator on a paper plate and left again.

"What are we going to do about Max?" said Annette.

"Send him packing," said Richard.

"Do you really think it's going to be that easy?" said Annette.

"Yes. Sonia knows I cannot stand dogs. Neither can her mother. We've been through this before. She accepts it."

Annette turned from Richard. "Well, don't be too sure," she said.

Richard went into the living room.

"Guess what," said Sonia. "Max ate all the meatloaf." She waved the paper plate at him.

"Great, I was planning to have that for lunch," said Richard dryly. "Dr. Ackley, may I have a word with you?"

Sonia sat on the couch and dragged Max up onto her lap. Annette stood in the doorway, looking on. Sonia carefully tore two slits in the paper plate. Richard watched, his hands clasped behind his back. His thumbs were circling each other.

"About this dog—" said Richard. He walked across the room.

"You're gorgeous," said Sonia to Max. She pushed each of Max's ears through a slit in the plate. "There!" she said. "Now you have a hat!"

Max licked her. She licked him back. Richard made an unpleasant face.

"That hat looks great!" said Annette. "Where's the camera?"

Richard began again. "I know you really like the dog, but he belongs somewhere."

"With me," said Sonia. "He's been abandoned. He came to me. He passed all the other houses. He's supposed to be mine." She pulled each ear out a little farther.

Richard turned and paced. "I don't like saying no," he said. "It's harder for me to say no than it is for other fathers because we only see each other on weekends."

Annette opened the closet to look for the camera.

"But," said Richard, "since we only see each other on weekends, I have more reasons to say no than other fathers." He put his hands in his pockets and jingled some change. "Number one: I don't like dogs and they don't

like me." Richard pulled out a couple of coins and tossed them in the air. He caught them. "Number two: While you're at your mother's apartment, the dog becomes my responsibility."

Annette looked at him.

"And Annette's," he added. "Anyhow, since you're at your mother's house all week long, and I would have to walk the dog—"

"I could walk him," said Annette.

"—and feed him *and* pay the vet bills—" He dropped the coins into his pocket and glanced at Annette. "I feel that it's my decision." Richard looked at Sonia. "I'm the father. And I'm saying no."

Max jumped down. He shook off the hat and tore it up.

"You call me Dr. Ackley because you *know* I am planning to be a veterinarian," said Sonia, "yet you don't want me to have experience in the field by having pets."

"You're being unfair," said Richard. "I do let you have pets. Even though they abuse me. Have you forgotten this?" He displayed a small scar on the side of his finger.

"How could I forget that?" said Sonia. "Fangs bit you."

"Yes, Fangs the Killer Lizard bit me," said Richard.

"Do you remember *how* it happened?" said Sonia.

A smile crept across Annette's face. She sat down and opened the newspaper.

"I don't recall, exactly," said Richard. "And it's a painful memory. Let's not go through it."

"Well, *I* remember exactly what happened," said Sonia. "You said that you were so fast you once won a pie-eating contest, and that when you were a kid people used to call you Swifty."

Richard pretended to be bored with the story.

"And," continued Sonia, "you said you bet you could put a termite down in front of Fangs before he could snap it out of your fingers."

Richard folded his arms and looked at the ceiling.

"I said, 'I bet you can't,' " said Sonia. "Annette said, 'Don't try it.' "

Richard stared over at Annette, who was behind the newspaper trying not to laugh.

"And," said Sonia, "Fangs bit you."

"I know you're laughing, Annette," said Richard as she turned the page. "Is this my fault, too?" He pulled up his pant leg. "What do you see here?" he asked.

"A white leg with blue hairs," said Sonia.

"Wrong!" said Richard. "A bruise. Laugh it up, Annette, at my expense!"

Annette folded the newspaper. "You were teasing Ms. Mackey, and she bit you."

"Teasing Mrs. Mackey!" said Richard. "I was getting mud off my zoris!"

"Mizzzzzzzz Mackey," said Sonia. "You were washing your feet in *her* pool, knowing she hates bare feet, and she bit you."

Richard threw up his hands. "*Her* pool. Now it's *her* pool. I built that for carp or goldfish!"

"*We* built that," said Annette.

"For whatever I wanted to put in it, and I chose a goose," said Sonia.

"No dog!" shouted Richard. He stalked into the kitchen, Annette and Sonia following him. "Send Weirdears home!" He crashed through the pot cupboard. "Where's the other half of the egg poacher?" He banged a griddle onto the stove. "No dog! Discussion closed!"

Sonia and Max went out on the stoop. They stood there a moment. Then Sonia bent down and gripped Max's nose with both hands. She looked into his eyes, frowning. "Go home!" said Sonia, knowing that he *was* home.

By the time breakfast was over and the dishes were done, Max had been sent away so many times by Richard that he moved off the stoop and into the hedge.

At noon, Richard called the pound. Sonia and Annette were listening.

Richard said, "You only keep strays five days? *Then* what? You must be kidding! Good-bye."

Sonia took the phone from him. She dialed her mother's number. "Hello, Mom?"

Annette left the room.

"Mom, can you and I keep a nice dog that Dad *hates* but I *love?*" Sonia glared at Richard and said to her mother, "Just a minute, someone's listening." She stepped into the closet with the telephone and closed the door. "Well, it would only be until we could locate the owner." Silence. "I *know* there are no dogs allowed in the apartment house, but nobody needs to know but us!" Silence, then mumbling. Sonia came out of the closet. "I know you were listening, Dad!"

"I admit it," said Richard. "And I'll tell you what. You really just want to locate the owner? Nobody told me that. Fair enough! You write a description of the dog. We'll run an ad in the classified section. We'll keep the dog as long as the pound would. By next weekend, we'll know something."

"Thanks, Dad!" Sonia gave him a hug.

Richard felt pleased with himself. He broke into a song.

Sonia ran to the freezer and took out four hot dogs. Then off she raced to her room for a pencil and paper. "Oops!" she said. She darted back into the kitchen and grabbed a handful of Cheerios out of the box. She opened the sliding door and threw the Cheerios onto the deck for Ms. Mackey. Then she said, "Dad? Will you please feed Fangs?"

"All right," said Richard. "I can deal with the lizard. Where's my leather glove?"

Sonia ran out the door. "Max!" she said. "Here!" She was breathless. "Here!" She fed him the hot dogs, one at a time.

Then Sonia wrote the ad:

> *Found. Brown dog with a white background. Wearing paper hat. Misbehaves. Has radish breath. Answers to the name "Weirdears."*
> *Call 233-7161.*

Sonia put the paper in her "DR. S. ACKLEY, D.V.M." pocket, and had a tumble with Max on the lawn. They spent the afternoon together, being pals. When it was

time to go to her mother's house, Sonia hugged Max and told him: "I'll see you again, so I won't say good-bye."

Max wagged his tail in a circle.

Sonia went into the house and handed Richard the ad.

"Sonia!" said Richard.

"Dr. Ackley," said Sonia.

"This doesn't even sound like the same dog! Max isn't a 'brown dog with a white background.' He's a white dog with brown spots!"

"Same thing," said Sonia.

"Also, Max doesn't misbehave. He's very polite," said Richard.

"Then why don't you like him?" said Sonia.

Richard turned the paper over, took a pen from his shirt, and clicked it once. "Let's see."

Sonia read over his shoulder as he wrote:

Found. White dog with brown spots. Vicinity Railroad Hill. Male. No tags. Medium-sized. Strange ears. Call 233-7161, through May 3rd.

"What does it mean, 'through May 3rd?' " she asked.

"After that," said Richard, "we're going to let someone adopt him."

Sonia fell into a swoon on the rug. "Us," she thought as she lay on the floor with her eyes shut.

"Now," said Richard. "Off we go to your mother's. We're already late."

As they were leaving, Annette picked up Max and waved his paw at Sonia. Sonia grinned.

"Ridiculous!" said Richard. He gave Annette a kiss. "Be right back!"

The week passed by slowly. Neither the newspaper ad nor calls to the pound and police station produced Max's owner. On Friday evening, Richard and Annette sat on the couch, waiting for Sonia to arrive. Max put his nose on Richard's knee.

Richard looked at Annette. "What does he want?" he asked.

"He's courting you," said Annette as Max licked Richard's hand.

"He's *tasting* me," said Richard. "He's thinking about sinking his teeth in my leg."

A horn beeped in the driveway. "Here she is now," Richard said. He went out on the stoop and waved.

"See you Sunday!" called Sonia's mother to Richard. She whizzed backward out of the driveway.

Sonia took the steps two at a time and ran past Richard. "Max!" she said. "I knew you'd be here!"

"Unfortunately," said Richard. "No owner."

"That's what I figured," said Sonia. "So"—she dug in her pack—"I wrote the ad"—she handed a note to Richard—"for Max to be adopted."

"Great!" said Richard. He felt relieved. "Then you *do* understand."

Neatly written, in multicolored ink, and decorated with pictures of iris and geraniums, Sonia had written:

> *Free. We don't want him. A weird dog. Blotchy-colored. Has ear problems. Tears hats. Lives in hedges. Wags his tail in a circle instead of up and down. Call 233-7161.*

"Sonia!" said Richard.

She pointed to the name on her pocket.

"Dr. Ackley!" they both said at once.

"Nobody will want to adopt the dog if we say *this* in the paper."

"I know," said Sonia.

"Well, I also wrote one," said Richard. "I've already had it placed in tomorrow's paper." He opened his wallet and unfolded a piece of paper. He read it aloud:

> *"Free to a good home. Beautiful, medium-sized male, Shepherd-mix. Snow white with gorgeous brown dots. A real storybook dog that will be an excellent companion. Would prefer country environment. Loves children. Sweet disposition. Obedient. Expressive ears. Call 233-7161."*

Sonia looked at Richard and said, "Don't call me Dr. Ackley anymore." She turned and stormed into the kitchen. She unbuttoned her shirt and balled it up. She stuffed it into a box under the sink that was filled with bottles for the recycling center.

Very late that night, Sonia woke up. She slipped from her bed and found Max in the living room. She searched for some cowboy music on the radio. She held Max in her arms.

Annette appeared in the doorway. "What are you two doing up?"

"It might be our last night," said Sonia. "We're dancing. He weighs a ton." She turned off the radio and put Max down. "What are you doing up?"

"Restless," said Annette. "I keep hearing the trains—listen!" She put her finger to her lips. She closed her eyes. A train was drawing closer through the darkness to the station. They heard the lonesome wail of the train whistle. "It must be midnight. The freight is coming in."

Max whined softly. Sonia and Annette knelt beside him.

"I knew Mom or Dad wouldn't let me keep him," began Sonia. "Neither one of them likes dogs."

Max pushed his nose into Sonia's hand. She smoothed his whiskers. Annette said nothing.

"And," continued Sonia, "animals are better off in the country. It's just that I really believed that Max could be mine."

Annette didn't speak.

The freight train clattered away into the night. The whistle sounded faint and lost. They listened until it was gone.

Max sat with his neck stretched way back and his nose pointed up while they scratched his throat. He looked something like a stork.

"Max reminds me of Maxine," said Annette quietly.

"Really?" said Sonia. "What happened to Maxine?"

"Nobody knows for sure," said Annette. "She went off one day and didn't come back."

"Oh," said Sonia.

"We lived near the tracks—"

"Oh," said Sonia.

"My father was an engineer. One night he came home looking very sad." Annette's eyes were filling. "And my father told me—"

Sonia clutched Annette's hand. "Don't tell me. You don't have to say it."

"And my father told me that Maxine—"

Sonia hid her face in Max's neck.

"—that Maxine may have hopped a freight," said Annette, "and gone to Nashville to be a country western star."

Richard appeared in the doorway. "What's going on?" he said. "Who's going to Nashville?"

"No one!" said Annette. She stood up. "No one is going to Nashville!"

"Okay!" said Richard. "No one is going to Nashville!"

Max and Sonia got up.

Everybody went back to bed.

At nine o'clock the next morning the telephone rang. Sonia heard her father say, "Between East Railroad and Grant. About eight blocks west of the station. Come on over and see how you like him."

Richard hung up the phone. "They're coming this morning."

Sonia said nothing.

"I don't expect to be here," said Annette. "I have errands to do."

An hour later a pickup pulled into the driveway. Max barked. A woman got out of the truck and stretched. A man wearing green cowboy boots got out too, carrying a little girl wearing a felt jacket with cactuses on it and a red ballet skirt. She was holding an Eskimo Pie.

Richard walked down the steps with Max beside him. Sonia lingered in the doorway. Annette came out on the stoop, holding the box for the recycling center. Sonia's shirt was tucked between the bottles. Annette rested a corner of the box on the rail.

"Is this the dog?" said the woman. "He's a beauty!"

"Yes," said Richard.

The cowboy knelt down with his daughter. "Hey, partner!"

Max went over to them.

"Howdy boy!"

The little girl put out her hand, and Max licked it.

"Do you have a yard?" asked Richard.

"A ranch," said the cowboy. "With a lake." He patted Max. "What's your name, boy?"

"Max," said Richard.

"Why, you doggone pelican!" the cowboy told Max. "I have an uncle named Max!"

"We'll take him," said the woman. "For our little girl."

Sonia came out on the stoop. "Annette! Could you ask them about taking a goose, too?" She was blinking back tears. "And an alligator lizard?"

Annette heard a whistle. The train was coming in. "Listen!" she said. "No one is going to Nashville!" She pulled Sonia's shirt from the box. The box fell from her arms, and the bottles shattered on the cement.

"We're keeping the dog," said Annette. She almost choked on the words. She pressed the shirt into Sonia's hands.

Annette started down the steps. "We're keeping the dog!"

"Watch out for the glass!" said Richard.

Annette went to the little girl. "I'm sorry," she said. She picked up Max. She looked at Richard. "We're keeping this dog for our little girl." Tears were falling. She climbed the stairs.

"Okay! Okay! Watch out for the glass," said Richard.

Sonia was waiting. Annette put Max into her arms. "For Dr. Ackley," said Annette, "from your Wicked Stepmother and from your father, with love. Discussion closed."

THE DOG THAT WOULDN'T GO HOME

by Mavis Jukes

Early one morning in 1979, a dog appeared on my doorstep. For reasons known only to him, he decided he was mine—or I was his. When I shouted "Go home!" he hurried down the stairs and found a washcloth that had fallen from my clothesline. He carried it in his teeth to a spot near our hedge and lay down on it, refusing to budge.

I tried to ignore him. But, whenever I went outside, he would follow me—heeling beside me when I walked and sitting and panting beside me when I stopped. He was very protective; he curled his lips and showed his teeth to everyone who tried to come near me—especially my husband, Bob.

I put a number of ads in the newspaper, attempting to find the dog's true owner, but nobody answered. I wished I could have kept him, but having a dog that wouldn't let my husband near me would have presented problems. And it would have made life pretty miserable for my four cats, two dogs and sheep. None of them were allowed to enter the yard.

In the process of finding a good home for the dog, I must admit that I fell in love with him. I was flattered by his loyalty and affection. Plus, he had the greatest ears! He could wiggle them in a way I'd never seen any dog wiggle ears before. They looked like two fat flags waving on top of his head.

Eventually, with the help of the Humane Society, I found some nice people to take the dog in, a couple who lived on a fishing boat in Bodega Bay. But I hated to see him leave. I guess writing the book *No One Is Going to Nashville* was my way of holding on.

I have often felt that I owe my writing career to this dog who tried to adopt me, and for years I've been meaning to go to Bodega Bay and take him to a little seafood restaurant out there for lunch, and treat him to the captain's plate or a lobster tail.

Bob, of course, would have to stay home.

THINKING ABOUT IT

1 Tell about a time you or someone you know wanted something as much as Sonia wanted to keep Max.

2 *No One Is Going to Nashville*—what a strange title! Be the author for a moment and tell why you chose it.

3 Pick a family. It can be a real family, or a family from a story or TV show. How might that family solve the problem in *No One Is Going to Nashville?*

Another Book by Mavis Jukes
In *Like Jake and Me,* a fuzzy spider brings Alex and his new stepfather closer together.

We Don't Look Like Our Mom and Dad

BY HARRIET LANGSAM SOBOL

The Levins are a family. Eric and Joshua Levin are brothers. Their dog is named Melby.

Eric plays the cello, and Joshua loves to play Frisbee. Both boys are adopted, and both are Korean by birth.

The Levins adopted them when they were very young. Eric, who is ten years old, was only a few months old when he became part of the Levin family. Joshua was two and a half years old and is eleven now. Eric doesn't remember anything before he came to America, but Joshua has a few memories of his Korean foster family. Eric and Joshua are

brothers through adoption. Each boy has a different biological mother, but in the Levin household they are brothers.

The boys feel special about being Korean and a little different from their friends. They think about Korea and wonder what it's like. Their parents bought them a book that has pictures of Korea in it, and the boys enjoy looking through it. They continue to keep the clothing they wore when they came to America in special boxes, and they like to take out the tiny clothes and look at them.

Eric loves it when his father tells him about the day he arrived on the airplane from Korea. Mr. Levin was so anxious to hold Eric that he went straight to the gate at the airport, found the woman who had taken care of Eric on the trip, and took him in his arms right then and there. He knew it was Eric because the adoption agency had told him that Eric would be the only infant in the group.

When the boys ask why they were adopted, their parents tell them, "We needed to raise children, and you needed parents to raise you, so we are a perfect match."

"But why did you want to adopt Korean children?" they often ask next.

"There were a lot of children in Korea who needed parents, and the agency got us together."

Most of the time the boys don't think about being Korean. They are too busy playing with their friends and going to school. Eric spends much of his time practicing his cello or working with the computer in his classroom. He has shown some of his friends "Weeds Waving in the Wind," the computer program he created.

Joshua is a chess player and spends many winter afternoons playing matches at the library. He also likes to play kickball with his friend Frank. This year he worked very hard on a school report about Pelé. After school, Joshua and his friend Robert often play together in Joshua's backyard.

The Levins like to do things together. On weekends they go walking in the woods. They

also like to cook together. They have learned
how to make some Korean dishes. One of
their favorites is *bul-go-gee,* a sliced marinated
steak. They serve it with rice and *kim chee,* a
pickled cabbage dish that is a staple of the
Korean diet. The boys enjoy shopping at the
Korean market, and they help with the cutting
and slicing that is involved in the preparation
of the meal. The best part, of course, is
when the work is over and the family sits down
to dinner.

Joshua and Eric like to play together, but
occasionally they fight. Eric sometimes says,
"You're not my brother," when he is angry
with Joshua.

Their mother says, "In this family, you're
brothers."

When Eric was in nursery school, his friend asked him, "Can you see when you smile? Your eyes go away." The next day Eric worked very hard to try to keep his eyes open when he smiled, but he just couldn't.

The boys used to wonder why they look so different from their parents. They asked their father, "Why do you and Mommy have big noses and we have little noses? Who do we look like?" Their father explained that they look like their biological parents, but they didn't really understand. Now that they are older, they understand a little better.

When Eric was younger, he asked his mother where babies come from. His mother told him that babies grow inside their mothers. He asked, "Did I grow inside you?"

She answered, "No, you grew inside your biological mother, your Korean mother."

Eric became so angry he hit her and said, "You're a bad mother." As soon as he calmed down, his mother put her arms around him and told him how happy she and his father were to have adopted him and Joshua. She also told him how much they loved them and how pleased they were that they were their sons.

Lately Eric has been thinking a lot about his Korean mother. Why did she give him up for adoption? What did she look like and why didn't she keep him? If she were to come to this country, would she recognize him? Would she talk to him?

The boys have many questions like those, and some of the questions are hard to answer. No one knows what the boys' biological mothers look like, and no one knows why they had to give their babies up. Those are questions that simply cannot be answered.

"What is probably true," the Levins tell their sons, "is that your biological mothers cared about what would happen to you and couldn't take proper care of you. They must have felt sad for a long time after they gave you up for adoption."

Eric and Joshua know that their parents love them very much. They are part of a loving family. Their grandmother is also an important member of the family. She lives far away, but both boys look forward to her visits. They spend hours playing Hearts with her, and once in a while one of the boys wins a game.

Joshua and Eric love to talk about the day they became American citizens. Their father had said to them, "You are part of our family. Now it's time you adopt our country."

It was an important day, and Joshua and Eric got dressed in their best clothes to go to the courtroom. The courtroom was crowded with people who had come to be citizens. The judge spoke to them for a few minutes, and then everyone in the group pledged allegiance to the American flag. Joshua and Eric had been practicing the pledge with their parents for weeks.

Afterwards
the judge gave them
their citizenship papers,
and a woman from a local
organization gave them each an
American flag.

Although they have become American
citizens, the boys have kept Korean middle
names. Joshua's is Nam Sun and Eric's is
Hyun. Eric likes to tell his friend David that
he can't be President of the United States
because he is a naturalized citizen. "But I can
be President of Korea," he says.

Sometimes when the family goes out to
eat or to shop, people stare out of curiosity.
The boys used to be embarrassed, but
they are becoming accustomed to people's
questioning looks.

There
are many
Asian children who
have been adopted by
American families, but Joshua
and Eric aren't aware of it, because they
are the only adopted Asian children in their
school and neighborhood. There are other
Asian children in school, Koreans, Chinese,
and Japanese, but they all have Asian parents.

The Levins are not a typical family. No one
in the family is biologically related to any of the
others. Nevertheless they are a family because
they choose to be one. Like other families,
they live together and play together. Most
important, they share work and share love.

Thinking About It

1 You've just moved in next door to Eric and Joshua and have met them for the first time. What are your impressions of the two boys?

2 Which details from the selection show that the Levins really are a family?

3 The Levins saved Eric and Joshua's baby clothing to help the boys remember the time before they became the Levins' sons. What are some other baby things that people save? Why do you think they choose those things?

A Day With the Amish

by Linda Egenes

❖

We turn down a straight, narrow driveway bordered on the left by a half-acre garden, asleep for the winter. On the outside, the large white farmhouse and green farm buildings look much the same as other Iowa farms we have passed on the way, but the two black buggies, resting outside the four neatly painted farm buildings, assure us that we have come to the Amish home of the Herschberger family.

Mr. Herschberger greets us with a hearty handshake and warm smile. He wears the traditional Amish clothing—white shirt, suspenders, and plain denim pants. Inside the house, we meet

An Amish family farm has many barns for crops, equipment, and animals, as well as a large farmhouse.

Mrs. Herschberger and five of their eight children. Eddie, a shy boy of thirteen, and Andy Ray, nine, look like miniature versions of their father, minus the beard. Mrs. Herschberger and her three daughters—Mandy, age eleven; Erma, age sixteen; and Wilma, age eighteen—wear their hair gathered under white starched caps. Amish women do not cut their hair and wear the prayer cap at home and in public. Their simple, long-sleeve, high-neck dresses are fastened with straight pins instead of buttons or zippers.

We enter a long, large living room with a large quilting frame. Tiny stitches crisscross the green fabric that is stretched across the frame. We admire the quilt and a beautiful oak cabinet standing beside a large window. "That was my mother's," Mrs. Herschberger says.

We wonder how the house is heated. In one corner of the living room, an empty metal oil drum stands on its side, propped up by four legs above a bed of white stones. Wood is fed into it to heat the house. "Most winter days, it's almost too hot," Mrs. Herschberger notes.

How do they see at night? Mrs. Herschberger shows us a gas lamp, which she lights with a long kitchen match. The filament gives off a bright, powerful light. In the evenings, the family hangs a lamp from the hooks in the ceiling to light an entire room.

A wide doorway connects the master bedroom to the living room. Mr. Herschberger explains that he made the doorway purposely large so church services can be held in both rooms. He has plans to replace most of the wall with a sliding door to create one large room for Sunday meetings and other gatherings. Mr.

An Amish father and daughter, Kidron, Ohio.

An Amish family saying grace before a meal.

Herschberger explains that the Amish do not build church buildings for worship. Families take turns having services in their homes, barns, or sheds once every two weeks.

Mrs. Herschberger takes us upstairs to tour the rest of the house. One bedroom is for the two boys; another large one is for the three girls. The simple, neatly arranged rooms contain beds, dressers, and closets. There are no toys in the rooms, no rugs on the floor,* and no pictures on the walls. Amish children amuse themselves by reading or playing outdoor games

*Some Amish have simple toys (wooden horses, jump ropes, etc.) and simple hooked rugs.

Amish boys loading sheaves of wheat onto a wagon.

talkative, the children are shy and quiet. Mandy reads a book while her parents talk.

Mrs. Herschberger speaks to Mandy in Pennsylvania Dutch, the mother tongue of the Amish, which is always spoken at home. Mandy sighs, puts down her book, and fetches Mrs. Herschberger's glasses. We comment on the polite behavior of the children, and Mr. Herschberger says with a smile, "Well, they're good around company."

We learn that only Mandy, Andy Ray, and Eddie are still in school; Eddie, grade eight, will graduate this spring. Erma and Wilma help their mother with the farm and house work. Besides furrowing the half-acre garden and corn fields with a horse and plow, they manually collect thirteen thousand eggs twice each day from

such as skating or kick the can.

After the tour, we settle into straight-back chairs for a chat, nibbling from bowls of tender popcorn made from the corn grown in their garden. The five children sit on a couch beside their parents. While Mr. and Mrs. Herschberger are outgoing, jovial, and

Amish children at a one-room school relax during the noon lunch period.

their fifteen thousand-bird hen house.

Mr. Herschberger offers to take us on a buggy ride and sends Andy Ray out to hitch up one of their fifteen horses. After we have all been properly introduced to June, the shaggy black horse that will draw the buggy, Mr. Herschberger heads June onto the highway. The ride is a little bumpy because the wheels are made of steel.

A small white building is standing by the side of the highway. "That's our schoolhouse," Mr. Herschberger says. He ties June to a hitching post inside the pony shed and leads us inside. Fourteen Amish children from grades one to eight attend the one-room school. The old-fashioned wooden desks, complete with inkwells and attached seats, look well used. They are arranged in neat rows. A reciting bench is placed next to the teacher's desk, so one class can recite its lessons while others work on assignments. Written on the black-board is a psalm from the Bible. A sign advises, "If you have something to say about someone else, you should say it as if he were listening." A wood stove provides the heat, and the only plumbing is a sink for washing hands. An outhouse stands at the edge of the schoolyard.

After we return to the farm and take a tour of the barn, Mrs. Herschberger invites us back into the house, where the children have been taking turns churning the handle on the ice cream maker. As we sit with Mr. and Mrs. Herschberger in the kitchen, savoring the rich flavor of homemade vanilla ice cream, there is a slight commotion in the dining room, and the children begin singing a song they learned in school.

After the singing is over, we get ready to start home. The Herschbergers bid us good-bye at the door as we leave, laden with bags of homegrown popcorn, jars of dill pickles, and a taste of the simple charm of Amish life.

Thinking About It

1. You've been assigned to interview the Herschbergers for your school newspaper. What is the first thing you ask them?

2. What are some traditions the Amish parents are passing on to their children?

3. You have traded families with an Amish child for a year. What are some ways your life is different now? What does the Amish child think of life with your family?

Yagua Days

by Cruz Martel
illustrations by Jerry Pinkney

I t was drizzling steadily on the Lower East Side. From the doorway of his parents' bodega, Adan Riera watched a car splash the sidewalk.

School had ended for the summer two days ago, and for two days it had rained. Adan wanted to play in East River Park, but with so much rain about the only thing a boy could do was watch cars splash by.

Of course he could help father. Adan enjoyed working in the bodega. He liked the smells of the fruits and the different colors of the vegetables, and he liked the way the mangós, ñames, and quenepas felt in his hands.

But today he would rather be in the park. He watched another car spray past. The rain began to fall harder.

Mailman Jorge sloshed in, slapping water off his hat. He smiled. "Qué pasa, Adan? Why the long face?"

"Rainy days are terrible days."

"No—they're wonderful days. They're yagua days!"

"Stop teasing, Jorge. Yesterday you told me the vegetables and fruits in the bodega are grown in panel trucks. What's a yagua day?"

"Muchacho, *this* day is a yagua day. And Puerto Rican vegetables and fruits *are* grown in trucks. Why, I have a truck myself. Every day I water it!"

Adan's mother and father came in from the back.

"Hola, Jorge. You look wet."

"I *feel* wetter. But it's a wonderful feeling. It's a yagua-day feeling!"

His mother and father liked Jorge. They had all grown up together in Puerto Rico.

"So you've been telling Adan about yagua days?"

"Sí. Mira! Here's a letter for you from Corral Viejo, where we all had some of the best yagua days."

Adan's father read the letter. "Good news! My brother Ulise wants Mami, Adan, and me to visit him on his finca for two weeks."

"You haven't been to Puerto Rico in years," said Mailman Jorge.

"Adan's *never* been there," replied his mother. "We can ask my brother to take care of the bodega. Adan will meet his family in the mountains at last."

Adan clapped his hands. "Puerto Rico! Who cares about the rain!"

Mailman Jorge smiled. "Maybe you'll even have a few yagua days. Hasta luego. Y que gocen mucho!"

Tío Ulise met them at the airport in Ponce.

"Welcome to Puerto Rico, Adan."

Stocky Uncle Ulise had tiny blue eyes in a round, red face, and big, strong arms, but Adan, excited after his first plane ride, hugged Uncle Ulise even harder than Uncle Ulise hugged him.

"Come, we'll drive to Corral Viejo." He winked at Adan's father. "I'm sorry you didn't arrive yesterday. Yesterday was a wonderful yagua day."

"You know about yagua days too, tío Ulise?"

"Sure. They're my favorite days."

"But wouldn't today be a good yagua day?"

"The worst. The sun's out!"

In an old jeep, they wound up into the mountains.

"Look!" said Uncle Ulise, pointing at a river jumping rocks. "Your mother and father, Mailman Jorge, and I played in that river when we were children."

They bounced up a hill to a cluster of bright houses. Many people were outside.

"This is your family, Adan," said Uncle Ulise.

Everyone crowded around the jeep. Old and young people. Blond-, brown-, and black-haired people. Dark-skinned and light-skinned people. Blue-eyed, brown-eyed, and green-eyed people. Adan had not known there were so many people in his family.

Uncle Ulise's wife Carmen hugged Adan and kissed both his cheeks. Taller than Uncle Ulise and very thin, she carried herself like a soldier. Her straight mouth never smiled—but her eyes did.

The whole family sat under wide trees and ate arroz con gandules, pernil, viandas and tostones, ensaladas de chayotes y tomates, and pasteles.

Adan talked and sang until his voice turned to a squeak. He ate until his stomach almost popped a pants button.

Afterward he fell asleep under a big mosquito net before the sun had even gone down behind the mountains.

I n the morning Uncle Ulise called out, "Adan, everyone ate all the food in the house. Let's get more."

"From a bodega?"

"No, mi amor. From my finca on the mountain."

"You drive a tractor and plow on the mountain?"

Tía Carmen smiled with her eyes. "We don't need tractors and plows on our finca."

"I don't understand."

"Vente. You will."

Adan and his parents, Aunt Carmen, and Uncle Ulise hiked up the mountain beside a splashy stream.

Near the top they walked through groves of fruit trees.

"Long ago your grandfather planted these trees," Adan's mother said. "Now Aunt Carmen and Uncle Ulise pick what they need for themselves or want to give away or sell in Ponce."

"Let's work!" said Aunt Carmen.

Sitting on his father's shoulders, Adan picked oranges.

Swinging a hooked stick, he pulled down mangós.

Whipping a bamboo pole with a knife tied to the end, he chopped mapenes from a tall tree.

Digging with a machete, he uncovered ñames.

Finally, gripping a very long pole, he struck down coconuts.

"How do we get all the food down the mountain?" he asked.

"Watch," said Aunt Carmen. She whistled loudly.

Adan saw a patch of white moving in the trees. A horse with a golden mane appeared.

Uncle Ulise fed him a guanábana. The horse twitched his ears and munched the delicious fruit loudly.

"Palomo will help us carry all the fruit and vegetables we've picked," Adan's mother said.

Back at the house, Adan gave Palomo another guanábana.

"He'll go back up to the finca now," his father said. "He's got all he wants to eat there."

Uncle Ulise rubbed his knee.

"Qué te pasa?" asked Adan's mother.

"My knee. It always hurts just before rain comes."

Adan looked at the cloudless sky. "But it's not going to rain."

"Yes, it will. My knee never lies. It'll rain tonight. Maybe tomorrow. Say! When it does, it'll be a yagua day!"

I n the morning Adan, waking up cozy under his mosquito net, heard rain banging on the metal roof and coquies beeping like tiny car horns.

He jumped out of bed and got a big surprise. His mother and father, Uncle Ulise, and Aunt Carmen were on the porch wearing bathing suits.

"Vámonos, Adan," his father said. "It's a wonderful yagua day. Put on your bathing suit!"

In the forest he heard shouts and swishing noises in the rain.

Racing into a clearing, he saw boys and girls shooting down a runway of grass, then disappearing over a rock ledge.

Uncle Ulise picked up a canoelike object from the grass. "This is a yagua, Adan. It fell from this palm tree."

"And this is what we do with it," said his father. He ran, then belly-flopped on the yagua. He skimmed down the grass, sailed up into the air, and vanished over the ledge. His mother found another yagua and did the same.

"Papi! Mami!"

C·71

Uncle Ulise laughed. "Don't worry, Adan. They won't hurt themselves. The river is down there. It pools beneath the ledge. The rain turns the grass butter-slick so you can zip into the water. That's what makes it a yagua day! Come and join us!"

That day Adan found out what fun a yagua day is!

C·73

Two weeks later Adan lifted a box of mangós off the panel truck back in New York.

"Hola, muchacho! Welcome home!"

Adan smiled at Mailman Jorge. "You look sad, compadre."

"Too much mail! Too much sun!"

"What you need is a yagua day."

"So you know what a yagua day is?"

"I had six yagua days in Puerto Rico."

"You went over the ledge?"

"Of course."

"Into the river?"

"Sí! Sí! Into the river. Sliding on yaguas!"

"Two-wheeled or four-wheeled yaguas?"

Adan laughed. "Yaguas don't have wheels. They come from palm trees."

"I thought they came from panel trucks like mine."

"Nothing grows in trucks, Jorge. These mangós and oranges come from trees. The gandules come from bushes. And the ñames come from under the ground. Compadre, wake up. Don't *you* know?"

Mailman Jorge laughed. "Come, campesino, let's talk with your parents. I want to hear all about your visit to Corral Viejo!"

Spanish Word List

arroz con gandules (ah-ROHZ kon ghan-DOO-les) · rice with pigeon peas

bodega (boh-DEG-ah) · Puerto Rican grocery store

buenos días (BWEN-noss DEE-ahs) · good day or hello

campesino (kham-peh-SEE-noh) · country boy

compadre (kom-PA-dreh) · pal

coquies (koh-KEES) · tree frogs

Corral Viejo (koh-RALL vee-YEH-hoh) · old corral

ensaladas de chayotes y tomates (en-sah-LAH-dahs deh chah-YOH-tehs ee toh-MAH-tehs) · salads of chayotes (squash-like vegetables) and tomatoes

finca (FEEN-kah) · plantation

guanábana (ghwah-NAH-bah-nah) · a sweet, pulpy fruit, slightly smaller than a football, covered with prickly skin

hasta luego (AH-stah loo-WEH-goh) · till we meet again; good-bye

hola (OH-la) · hello

mami (MAH-mee) · mommy

mangó (mahn-GO) · a sweet, tropical fruit, golden when ripe

mapenes (mah-PEN-nehs) · breadfruit

mi amor (mee ah-MOHR) · my love

mira (MEE-rah) · look

muchacho (moo-CHA-choh) · boy

ñame (NYAH-meh) · a tropical root vegetable
similar to a potato

Palomo (pah-LOH-moh) · dove

papi (PAH-pee) · daddy

pasteles (pahs-TELL-ehs) · Puerto Rican
dumplings

pernil (pehr-NEEL) · roast pork butt

plátano (PLAH-ta-noh) · a tropical fruit similar
to a banana

qué pasa? (keh PAH-sah) · what's happening?

qué te pasa? (keh teh PAH-sah) · what's
the matter?

quenepa (keh-NEH-pah) · a grape-sized fruit
with a hard, green peel

sí (see) · yes

tía (TEE-ah) · aunt

tío (TEE-oh) · uncle

tostones (tohs-TOH-nehs) · fried green
plantains

vámonos (BAH-moh-nohs) · let's go

vente (BEN-teh) · come on

viandas (vee-AHN-dahs) · general term for
Puerto Rican vegetables

y que gocen mucho (ee keh GOH-sen
MOO-choh) · and have fun!

yagua (JAH-gwah) · the outer covering of a
sprouting palm frond

Thinking About It

1 What are yagua days? Why do the characters in the story remember them so happily? What kind of days do you remember so fondly you could give them a special name?

2 You've recently visited Puerto Rico with your friend, Adan. What did you do while you were there?

3 From what you've found out about Puerto Rico in this story, tell why you would or wouldn't like to take a vacation there.

I'm the Big Sister Now

by Michelle Emmert
Illustrations by Gail Owens

me taking a ride
with Amy.

All about Amy

When my sister Amy was born, my mom and dad knew right away that she was going to be a special little girl. Part of her brain did not work because she did not get enough oxygen during birth. This kind of brain damage is called cerebral palsy.

Some people with cerebral palsy have a limp or a hand that is crooked at the wrist so they can't hang onto things. Or maybe they are a little hard to understand when they talk. Some others who can't walk can still run their own wheelchairs. But Amy is severely handicapped. She cannot sit up, use her hands, walk, talk, read, write, or do anything a normal child can do. She has always been in a wheelchair that was made just for her.

Even though she can't do very many things, she is still a great sister, and I would like to tell you about her.

How I Feel about Amy

Amy was five when I was born. I
didn't know then that she was different from
any other big sister. I liked being near her.
She made sounds like me, and I felt happy and
safe beside her.

After I grew out of my youth bed, I
told my mom and dad that Amy was scared
and needed me. But I was the one who was
really afraid, so I started sleeping
with Amy. When I had a bad dream
or was scared of the dark, I just
cuddled up to her, and we both
went to sleep.

Now I'm not scared of the dark anymore, but I still like to be with Amy. Sometimes I think she is really better than other big sisters. My friends say their older sisters are always bossing them around. Amy never tells me what to do, and she always listens.

Amy gets sick a lot. Once she was so sick we thought she might die. I know she won't live as long as I will, and that makes me sad. I wonder when she will die, and how. I hope it won't hurt her when she dies.

It's lonely at night when Amy is in the hospital, and we are all glad when she comes home. When Amy is well, I don't worry about her.

I don't think I'm jealous of the time Mom and Dad spend with Amy because she can't help being sick. When she's okay, they do special things with me.

As I grow older, I get bigger, like most kids do. But Amy doesn't grow very fast. She is fourteen and looks like she's only five or six. I'm nine, but I can hold Amy or even carry her if I'm very careful. Mom says I've become the big sister because I'm taller and because I help Amy to feel happy and safe. Being her big sister makes me feel good inside too.

How Others Feel about Amy

One time when I was little, Mom, Amy, and I went to the park. A guy on a huge motorcycle pulled up. He had long, greasy hair and a jacket with the name of a gang on it. My mom was worried he'd cause trouble, and she couldn't see a policeman or anyone else around. But when he got close, Mom saw he had tears in his eyes. He said, "Can I do anything for your little girl?" My mom was relieved and answered all his questions. Amy always brings out the best in people.

When I was about seven, we went to a basketball game. A couple of girls started staring at Amy. I went over to Amy and hugged her. Then I glared at the girls, and they went away. Amy does not like people staring or pointing at her; we think she gets uncomfortable. But we do not mind having people ask questions because it shows they care and are interested. People usually say things like, "Was she born the way she is?" or "Can she walk or talk?" Sometimes they ask whether she's happy or sad when she makes loud noises, or why she always has her mouth open.

I can answer most questions. Her noises are happy or sad depending on what is happening, and she cannot close her mouth completely because of the way it is formed.

My family went to my grandma and grandpa's church last year, and someone we didn't know said, "Merry Christmas, Amy." We couldn't figure out how he knew her. But then later we noticed that Amy's wheelchair had a nametag tied on. It made us feel good that people cared enough about Amy to include her.

Christmas at Grandma's and Grandpa's church.

Amy and me cuddling in bed when I was little.

Sometimes when I go to the pool, Amy will come. She is pretty light and can float without a life jacket if people hold their hands under her head. Little kids five or six years old will float her by keeping her head up out of the water and pulling her around the pool. Sometimes they argue over whose turn it is to float Amy. She laughs a lot while she floats and smiles at the person pulling her. Mom sits right nearby so she can help if Amy starts to slip under.

Amy started going to a special school when she was one year old. All the kids there are handicapped, but in different ways. Some of them can walk a little or play with toys by themselves. Some kids learn to feed themselves and to use the bathroom. The kids who can move their hands but cannot talk learn sign language. With the teachers' help, some kids can paint pictures. There are special exercise mats and balls in the classroom and a "standing board" to help kids stand in front of a desk. Amy likes to play in a big playpen filled with styrofoam.

C·87

Teachers from other rooms like to visit Amy, especially when they're sad or lonely. Amy makes people feel happy and important. She is very pretty, and she almost always smiles when you talk to her. Her eyes tell you how much she likes life, and you think, "If she's not sad, then I shouldn't be, because I can do a lot of things." And Amy is a very good listener. You can tell her secrets, and you know she won't tell anyone. She'll listen as long as you want to talk without telling you she's too busy or that what you're saying is stupid. You always feel better after you talk to her.

How to Take Care of Amy

Amy's brain damage was severe, and she cannot even hold her head up by herself. We hold it up for her when we are playing with her, and when she sits in her wheelchair, the high back holds her head up. Her wheelchair also tilts back a little instead of sitting perfectly straight, and that stops her head from falling forward. We push her around the house in the wheelchair and go for long walks outside.

Until she was thirteen, Amy ate regular food, except blended. But when she swallowed her food, she would often choke. Then the food would go down into her lungs instead of into her stomach, and she would get very sick with pneumonia. She would start breathing loudly, and it seemed as if she was working very hard just to push the air in and out. She would also get mucus in her throat, and we had to use a suction machine to get it out. Many times we couldn't make her well at home, and she would have to go into the hospital. Now she has a gastrostomy tube that we feed her through. It is about the size of a pencil and goes straight into her stomach. We get Isocal, a special liquid food, at a drugstore, and she is healthier now than when she ate regular food.

Amy has a special bathtub that my dad and grandpa built in her bedroom. She catches a cold very easily, so when it's time for her bath, we make her room nice and warm. Then we just move her from the bathtub to her dressing table, and we can bundle her up in towels. The tub is higher from the floor than most tubs so whoever bathes Amy will not have to bend too far. It is very shallow because Amy is too heavy to lift out of a deep tub. Dad and Grandpa put a regular toilet under the tub, and we can rinse her diapers right away. Because there is a lot to do to make Amy comfortable, we are trying to make taking care of her easy.

Amy has a big waterbed in her room. Since she is thin and can't roll over by herself, it would hurt to lie on a regular bed all night. But with her waterbed, she feels like she's floating at the pool, and she doesn't get tired of lying in the same place. A heater in the bed keeps her warm and cozy all the time. My friends and I like to bounce Amy on her bed. We get it rolling like big waves, and she slides back and forth and rolls from side to side. Sometimes she laughs so hard she can hardly get her breath, and we have to stop for a minute. Then we do it again!

If Amy starts crying, I hold her and talk or read to her, and she stops. Sometimes when I babysit Amy, I play with her. If I cough, sneeze, snore, clap, slam drawers, or move my head up and down, Amy laughs. We don't know why she laughs at these weird things, but she does.

Amy likes to watch me do things like play the violin, carve pumpkins, and decorate the Christmas tree. When I send cards to good friends, I help Amy sign the cards with an *X* or I help her write her name. I put the pen in her fingers, and then I take hold of her hand and move it to make the letters we want. It doesn't look quite as good as if I did it myself, but our friends think it's neat, and so do I. Even though I am younger, I like taking care of Amy.

MY ADOPTED GRANDPA

BY AMIE WORTMAN, AGE 12

It was party time! For weeks, the neighborhood children had anticipated the bright party hats, horns, and favors, along with yummy cake (chocolate, I hope) with lots of ice cream on top. The day was here and children of various ages took their places at the neatly decorated table. One chair was left for the guest of honor—not another child, but for Grandpa Bob. It was his eightieth birthday. He had made it clear he only wanted children there. That way he could just be himself.

After a lively chorus of "Happy Birthday," we all helped blow out the candles on the cake. (By the way, it *was* chocolate!) As soon as it was served with a generous double scoop of chocolate chip ice cream, Grandma Irene poured strawberry pop for each of us.

After we had all eaten our fill and waddled into the living room, we were each handed a sheet of drawing paper. We could color and draw anything we wanted, knowing Grandpa would keep it for his scrapbook as a unique gift from each of us. Then, do you know what? We had a balloon-stomping contest. I was stunned! Mom never, never let me pop balloons, but here was my golden opportunity to make up for lost time. Grandpa said, "Go!" and he and Grandma poured inflated balloons on the floor. A spinning blur of feet followed. (We couldn't use our hands.) BANG! Fast Charlie got one! I aimed for the orange one and POOF, it shot up into the air without breaking. However, I nailed it on the down-draft and after a loud POP, a quick look of satisfaction spread across my face. I, Tricky Tess, had gotten one! We moved on as Timmy, Andrea, Stacey, Derek, and Amie held their own. Eventually, we lost track of how many we all broke, but when we were done, deflated pieces of various colors of balloons lay strewn on the floor. We collapsed into a giggling heap of laughter and exhaustion.

After gaining a second wind, we played the ever-popular "Pin the Tail on the Donkey" game. We all took our turns. Since Stacey and I were only about three feet tall, the donkey "walked on his tails." Derek and Amie were taller, so the donkey's tail "flew over him." Then it was Charlie's turn. It was close! In a hushed silence, Andrea was blindfolded and ZOWIE, she got it just right!

Grandpa then opened his presents. He sure got lots of candy. We all knew Grandpa had a sweet tooth as big as an elephant's tusk!

Time soon came for us to go home and after a last round of strawberry pop and hugs and kisses, all the kids went home, but me. I loved Grandpa so much, I just had to tell him one more time when it was quiet and I was sure he'd hear. He isn't my real grandpa, you see. My real grandparents all live nearly four hundred miles away and I don't get to see them very often. Until four years ago, when we moved next door to Bob and Irene, I envied most other children because their grandparents could visit school and come to their programs, but there was always an

empty place where mine should have been. Then one day, when Mom was "too busy," Dad was working on the car, and my brother and sister seemed to be nowhere in sight, Bob came over to talk to me outside. His gentle nature was quickly apparent, and he wasn't too busy and he wasn't in a hurry. He had time for just me! Our friendship became a closeness I longed for and he soon came over nearly every day. Mom and Dad and the rest of my family looked forward to his visits as much as I did. He soon became known as "Grandpa Bob."

Grandpa visits us when we're sick, carries an endless supply of quarters for sweet surprises, sometimes plays cards with us, and above all else, he's just around to listen and talk. Now I understand when Mom says, "There's growth in listening and wisdom in love."

We love my "real" grandparents, as no one can ever take their place, but in our hearts there's a special place just for Grandpa Bob. Just think of the memories created each day we spend together. Thanks Grandpa Bob!

THINKING ABOUT IT

1 How did reading *I'm the Big Sister Now* make you feel? Did any parts surprise you? Were any parts particularly interesting or uninteresting?

2 Both "My Adopted Grandpa" and *I'm the Big Sister Now* are about real people and things that really happened. How might these selections be different if they were fiction?

3 You have been hired to write a book about someone you know. What person do you choose? Why? What do you do to start your research?

Memories of Family

by Eloise Greenfield

*Eloise Greenfield, her mother, and
her grandmother worked together to tell
the story of their family through three
generations. In Childtimes each woman
tells some memories of her childhood
and growing-up years. The excerpt that
follows is from the last third of the book
in which Eloise Greenfield tells her part
of the family's story.*

I'm Born

They say Mrs. Rovenia Mayo delivered more than a hundred babies in and around Parmele. I was one of them.

Mama wasn't expecting me until the end of the month, but I fooled her—I was ready to see the world on the seventeenth of May. Daddy was downtown playing checkers in front of Mr. Slim Gordon's store, and Mama wanted to wait until he came home, but his mother told her, "That young'un ain't going to wait for nobody! I'm going to get Mrs. Mayo now!"

I was born at six o'clock that evening. My great-aunt Mary was there to welcome me, and both of my grandmothers, Williamann Little and Pattie Ridley Jones. My brother Wilbur was there, too, but he didn't think my arrival was anything to get excited about— Mrs. Mayo had helped him make his grand entrance just the year before.

When Daddy came home, I was all of half an hour old, and did I give him a surprise!

First Days

It's the first day of my life—my remembered life. I'm three years old, sitting on the floor with Mama. Cutting out a picture for my scrapbook, a picture of a loaf of bread. Cutting it out and pasting it in my book with the flour-and-water paste I had helped to make.

As far as I know, that was the day my life began.

My school life began two years later. Mama walked my cousin Vilma and me down P Street, through the open doors of John F. Cook School, and into Mrs. Staley's kindergarten class. Vilma and I were both scared. I was scared quiet; she was scared loud. I sat squeezed up in my chair, and Vilma screamed.

Chores

I used to think I had too much work to do. I had to make my bed, sweep the kitchen floor, and take turns washing the dishes. On Saturdays I'd dust and dust-mop my room and the living room. Once in a while I'd get a nickel for going to the store for a neighbor, and I helped Mama now and then with the laundry. Washing machines didn't have spin dryers then, and I had to take each piece of clothing out of the water and put it through the wringer so the rollers could squeeze the water out of it.

I used to think I had a lot of chores to do, but after Mama and Grandma told me what they did when they were children, mine didn't seem like anything.

THIS PAGE, top: *Mack Little, Lessie Jones Little, Williamann Little* (rear), *and Lessie's children* (front, left to right) *Wilbur, Vedie, Gerald, and Eloise, Parmele, 1941;* center: *Vera and Vedie Little, Langston Terrace, Washington, D.C., 1949;* left: *Eloise Little, 1932* OPPOSITE PAGE, left: *Eloise Little and Bobby Greenfield, 1948;* right: *Weston Little and children Gerald and Eloise, Langston Terrace, 1938*

Black Music

My brother Wilbur plays the music called jazz,
plays it on a stand-up bass in concert halls
and nightclubs all over the world. Black
music.

It has always been part of our lives. It's so
much a part of me that if you could somehow
subtract it from who I am, I would be a
stranger to myself. I wouldn't know how to
act. Spirituals, gospel, blues, rhythm-and-blues,
jazz. Black music.

When I was a little girl, I used to hear
Lillie singing, *"Some of these days, you're
gonna miss me, honey,"* bluesing it around
the house in her baby voice. At church, the
choir would sing the gospel, or take a white
hymn and bend it black. And the male quartet
at Grandma's church would stomp and shout
in harmony, looking hard at something in the
air, straining the veins in their necks, until
people here and there in the room got the
Holy Ghost and did their shout-dances, even
Grandma, a prim shouter, jumping up and
down in one spot.

We sang spirituals in the glee club at
school, and danced to black music on records,
and I don't think we could have fallen in love
if Billie Holiday hadn't sung "Lover Man" in
that sad, lonely way.

I don't know how many hours, all
together, I spent at the Howard Theater where

the great musicians came to play. I could never see a show just once, I'd have to stay there and see it at least one more time. We called it "bucking the show." My cousin Vilma and I bucked the show three times one Saturday, went to the one o'clock afternoon show and didn't get home until ten that night. Mama was waiting at the bus stop, worried to death, when we got off the bus. We just couldn't leave that music.

A New Sister

It was not long after my high school graduation that Mama told me about the baby she was going to have. I had two brothers and one sister, and I wanted another sister, but I wasn't going to get excited about a little thing like a baby. I was too grown up for that, I was almost a full-grown woman.

I had been only ten when Vedie was born, too young to always think about acting unconcerned. Right after she was born that morning, I had heard her crying. Four o'clock in the morning, I was asleep on my sofa bed in the living room, and she was upstairs crying that new-baby kind of crying, *a-laaagh! a-laaagh! a-laaagh!* I woke right up. I kept my eyes closed, though, until I heard the doctor leave, and then I went upstairs to look at my baby sister.

But that had been a long time before. This time was going to be different. At least, that's what I thought. Then we started getting the house ready for the new baby, deciding where to put the crib, and buying clothes. And we had a long family meeting to pick out a name. For a girl, we chose Vera, and I can't remember the name we chose for a boy because we never had to use it.

I was almost eighteen when Vera was born, but that didn't stop me from running to the window and yelling to a friend, "Hey! I got a new sister!" I forgot I was almost a full-grown woman.

Family

Family. All this running through my mind. . . .

Saturday Sunday mornings Daddy making pancakes big as the plate Daddy making fat hamburgers leftover stuffed with rice green peas enough for everybody. Hot nights leave our hot one room sleep till midnight pillows blankets grass bed beside the river. Lincoln Park evenings Mama other mothers bench-talk children playing.

Give Mama her lesson take my piano lesson teach Mama. Downtown Wilbur Gerald Eloise wait in the car have fun get mad have fun get mad. Go for a ride park car New York Avenue hill dark watch trains wave passengers

sitting in lighted window squares sliding by.
Gerald tell us the movie tell us show us be
the gangster be the good guy be the funny guy
tell us show us. Look out the window wait
wait snow stopping Daddy going to make
snow ice cream ready to eat without freezing.

Vedie little sister turning somersaults we
laugh. Vera baby sister fat baby laughing we
laugh. Play games I'm thinking of a word I'm
thinking of a word that starts with *S* guess
give a clue it's blue. Radio hear-see squeaking
door ghosts scary music. Parade take turns on
Daddy's shoulder watch the floats watch the
firemen march watch the horns watch the
sound of the bass drum.

Easter Monday picnic zoo dyed eggs
lionhouse popcorn polar bear picnic.
Merry-go-round Mama laughing. Sparrow's
Beach sun water-splashing sandy legs Mama
laughing. Mama laughing. . . .

All this running through my mind now,
running through my mind now.

Family.

I Remember

by Eloise Greenfield

I remember
walking down the street beside
Uncle Eddie's legs
taking a nap in Mama's lap
talking to the pigeons in the park
I remember
my fuzzy hat, my yellow cat
my potty pot
I remember a lot
but I wish I remembered
what I forgot

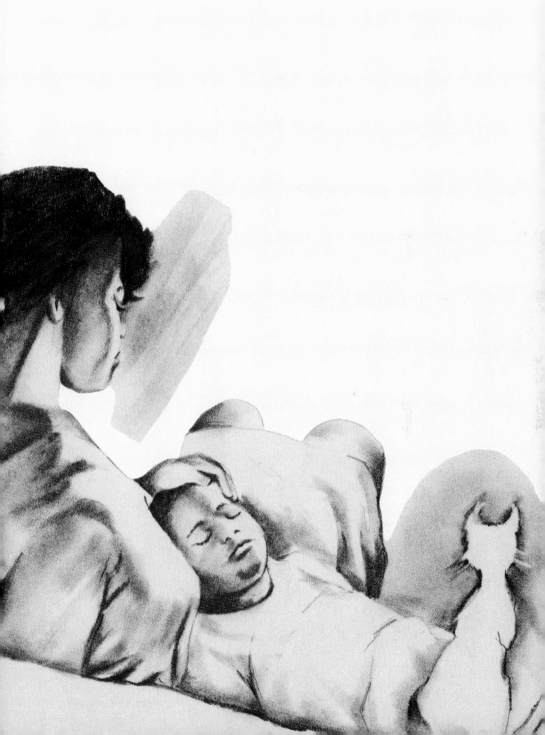

Grandma's Bones

by Eloise Greenfield

Grandma grew up
in the nineteen-forties
she can still do the jitterbug
a dance they used to do
to the music of Duke Ellington,
Benny Carter, Count Basie
and such

she can spin a yo-yo
much better than I
and sometimes she puts
two sticks called bones
between the knuckles
of one hand and goes

clack clack clackety

clackety clack

clackety clackety clackety

clack clack

uh clackety clack

uh clackety clack

clack clack clackety

clackety clack!

My Daddy

by Eloise Greenfield

my daddy sings the blues
he plays it on his old guitar
my daddy sings the blues
and he plays it on an old guitar
he plucks it on the strings
and he sings about the way things are

he sings baby, baby, baby
I love you till the day I die
he sings baby, baby, baby
I love you till the day I die
well I hope you love me back
cause you know I don't want to cry

he sings 'Thaniel, 'Thaniel, 'Thaniel
boy I love you deed I do
he sings 'Thaniel, 'Thaniel, 'Thaniel
boy I love you deed I do
well you're a mighty fine fella
and son I'm so proud of you

my daddy sings the blues
he plays it on his old guitar
yeah my daddy sings the blues
and he plays it on that old guitar
he ain't never been on TV
but to me he's a great big star

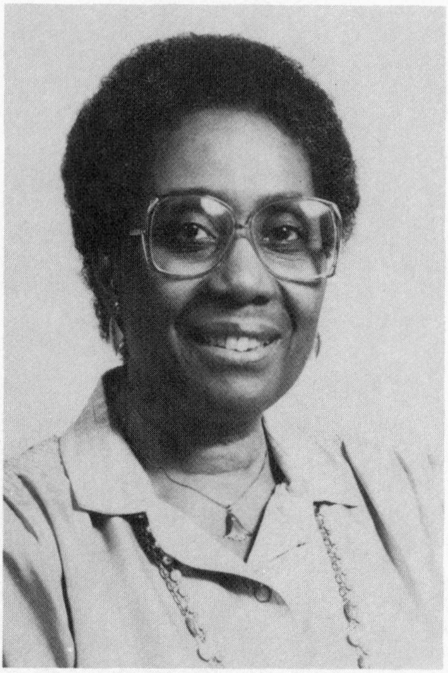

Writing for Children

by Eloise Greenfield

Eloise Greenfield

"Writing for children is fun, isn't it?" That's the question many adults ask me, all the while smiling and nodding their heads, as if to answer their own question, "Yes!"

I look at their faces before I answer. If their eyes are dreamy, looking back to a happy time when they were children reading their favorite books, I know they're too busy listening to their memories to hear what I have to say. Still, I answer them, but in the fewest possible words.

"Sometimes it is," I say, and I let my smile be the period at the end of the sentence.

But, if curiosity shines in the questioners' eyes, I tell them the whole truth—that writing is fun and serious and interesting and worrisome and exhausting and exciting and challenging and painful and satisfying and magical.

Talk About a Family began in a magical way. I was sitting on my sofa, daydreaming, letting my mind go wherever it chose to go, and I suddenly saw in my imagination a girl riding down the street on her bicycle. It was an autumn day, and as she passed under a tree, a leaf fell on her shoulder and stayed there for just a moment before it blew away.

"It had to mean good luck." Those were the words that came with the picture I saw. Who was this girl? What was her life like, and why did she need good luck? I decided to create a world for her.

When the idea for *Childtimes* came, I was daydreaming again. It was a few years after my grandmother's death, and I was thinking about her, about the kind of person she was. Then my thoughts moved to the little stories she had written about her life and given to me.

I remembered that my mother had recently begun to write too, and it was as if my mother had stepped into an empty space between Grandma and me. In my mind's eye, the three of us formed a line. Grandma, Mama, me. I

wanted to write about that. I was excited. I got up and dialed my mother's number, and when I told her my idea, she was excited too.

It took us three years to finish the book.

In *Childtimes*, and in most of my work, music plays an important part. I almost think it weaves itself into my manuscripts when I'm not looking. The poems "My Daddy" and "Grandma's Bones," from the book *Nathaniel Talking*, are as much about my love for music as they are about Nathaniel's love for his family.

I love words too. Sometimes they make me laugh. Other times, I feel a kind of pain in struggling to find the right ones. But I keep struggling, because I want to do my best, and because I want children to have the best. And because I know that there will always be the gift of those special moments that are magical.

PULLING IT ALL TOGETHER

1 Read "Memories of Family," from *Childtimes* again. How do you think Eloise Greenfield feels about her family? How do you feel about her family now that you've read about it?

2 If three characters from three different stories in this book met on a long train ride, what might they tell each other about themselves and their families?

3 You are giving a party for all the characters in this book. What will people talk about at the party?

Another Book by Eloise Greenfield
The author shares more of her poems in *Honey, I Love and Other Love Poems.*

BOOKS TO ENJOY

The Family Under the Bridge
by Natalie Savage Carlson
Christmas plays a part in this story, set in Paris. A hobo meets a fatherless family in search of a home.

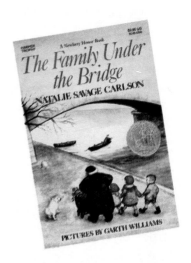

Sarah, Plain and Tall
by Patricia MacLachlan
Two prairie children are curious when their widowed father invites a young woman from far away to come visit them.

A Brown Bird Singing
by Frances Wosmek
Anego lives with the Veselka family. She fears the day when her Chippewa father will return and claim her. Will that day ever come? What will her father be like?

The Blossoms and the Green Phantom
by Betsy Byars
When Junior Blossom decides to invent a flying saucer, none of the other Blossoms take notice until the "Green Phantom" takes off and involves each family member in adventure.

The Hundred Penny Box

by Sharon Bell Mathis
Each penny in Aunt Dewbet's box symbolizes a memory which she shares with her great-great-nephew Michael. From Aunt Dew, Michael learns the value of keeping your memories tucked away in a safe place.

The Village of Round and Square Houses

by Ann Grifalconi
What would it be like to live in a village where the women live in round houses and the men in square houses? How does a volcano change this African village?

Me and My Family Tree

by Paul Showers
Why do family members sometimes look like each other? Who are our ancestors? This book explores heredity.

Grandparents' Houses: Poems about Grandparents

selected by Corrine Streich
Whether we're Japanese, American, or Zuni, we love and respect our grandparents. These poems are proof of our universal feelings.

LITERARY TERMS

Autobiography

An **autobiography** is the history of a person's life told by that person. In "Memories of Family" from *Childtimes,* Eloise Greenfield tells about her early life. What special times that she remembers does she choose to share with her readers?

Character

I'm the Big Sister Now gives you a chance to compare two sisters. One has cerebral palsy and the other does not. They are very different in many ways, yet they are also alike in some ways. The author lets you know that Amy can be happy or sad, like anyone else. You see that she likes to play at the swimming pool. What other things can you notice that show how Amy is like her sister, Michelle?

Narrative Nonfiction

I'm the Big Sister Now seems almost like fiction, but the opening section, "All About Amy," lets you know that it is nonfiction, a kind of nonfiction called **narrative nonfiction.** Narrative nonfiction such as *I'm the Big Sister Now* has a different tone from expository nonfiction such as "The Oldest Street in Town," which is straightforward explanatory writing that could not be mistaken for fiction.

Point of View

"Memories of Family" is written from Eloise Greenfield's point of view. She tells the story of her life using words such as *I* and *my*. These words tell readers that the story is being told in the first person point of view. *I'm the Big Sister Now* is also told from the first person point of view. *We Don't Look Like Our Mom and Dad* is different. Someone else is telling the story, not one of the boys. It is written from the third person, *they*, point of view.

Setting

The setting of *Yagua Days* is very important. Through words and pictures, you experience the New York City setting at the beginning of the story. When Adan and his family visit relatives in Puerto Rico, the setting changes dramatically. You experience mountains and a river and tall palm trees. You experience steamy, wet yagua days.

GLOSSARY

Vocabulary from your selections

a·ban·don (ə ban′dən), **1** to give up entirely: *We abandoned the idea of a picnic because of the rain.* **2** to leave without intending to return to; desert: *The crew abandoned the sinking ship. verb.*

a·ban·doned (ə ban′dənd), deserted: *The children played in the abandoned house. adjective.*

a·buse (ə byüz′ *for 1 and 3;* ə byüs′ *for 2 and 4*), **1** to make bad or wrong use of: *Don't abuse the privilege of using the library by talking too loud.* **2** a bad or wrong use: *The people hated the wicked king for his abuse of power.* **3** to treat cruelly or roughly: *The children abused the dog by throwing rocks at it.* **4** cruel or rough treatment: *I stopped their abuse of the dog.* 1,3 *verb,* **a·bus·es, a·bused, a·bus·ing;** 2,4 *noun.*

a·dop·tion a·gen·cy, a service organization that places children without homes into new homes: *The adoption agency told Mark he could have information about his birth mother when he was older. noun.*

al·le·giance (ə lē′jəns), devotion to someone or something; loyalty: *I pledge allegiance to the flag. We owe our friends our allegiance. noun.*

A·mish (ä′mish), **1** a group of people who have descended from the followers of Jacob Amman, a Swiss bishop of the 1600s: *My friends Sue and Jan are Amish.* **2** having to do with Amish people or customs: *We often shop for fresh food in the Amish community near our home.* 1 *noun,* 2 *adjective.*

Amish (definition 2)—**Amish** buggies

A·sian (ā′zhən), **1** of Asia; having something to do with Asia or its people; from Asia: *Fang Li teaches an Asian Studies course at the local college.* **2** a person born or living in Asia. 1 *adjective,* 2 *noun.*

bass (bās), **1** the lowest singing voice of a man. **2** a singer with such a voice. **3** a part sung by such a voice. **4** an instrument playing such a part: *Edward plays the bass in a jazz band. noun, plural* **bass·es.**

bi·o·log·i·cal (bī/ə loj/ə kəl), **1** of living things: *He is engaged in biological studies.* **2** having to do with biology: *Kara and Kim are each other's adopted sisters, not biological sisters. adjective.*

brain dam·age, a severe injury to the brain that takes place before, during, or after birth. People with brain damage often need special schooling and care: *Carrie's brother has brain damage that has made it difficult for him to learn to speak clearly. noun.*

de·ci·sion (di sizh/ən), **1** a deciding; judgment; making up one's mind: *I have not yet come to a decision about buying a coat.* **2** firmness and determination: *She is a woman of decision who makes up her mind what to do and then does it. noun.*

driz·zle (driz/əl), **1** to rain gently, in very small drops like mist: *The constant drizzle made everyone gloomy.* **2** very small drops of rain like mist. **1** *verb,* **driz·zles, driz·zled, driz·zling;** **2** *noun.*

fur·row (fėr/ō), **1** a long, narrow groove or track, as one cut in the earth by a plow. **2** cut furrows in. **3** to make wrinkles in: *The old woman's face was furrowed with age.* **1** *noun,* **2,3** *verb.*

furrow (definition 1)

a hat	i it	oi oil	ch child	ə stands for:
ā age	ī ice	ou out	ng long	a in about
ä far	o hot	u cup	sh she	e in taken
e let	ō open	ů put	th thin	i in pencil
ē equal	ô order	ü rule	ŦH then	o in lemon
ėr term			zh measure	u in circus

gath·er (gaŦH/ər), **1** to bring or come together; collect: *He gathered his books and left for school. A crowd gathered to hear the speech.* **2** to pick: *He gathered a bouquet of flowers from the garden.* **3** to get or gain little by little: *The train gathered speed as it left the station.* **4** to put together in the mind; conclude: *I gather from the excitement that something important has happened.* **5** to pull together in folds: *The dressmaker gathered the skirt at the waist.* **6** one of the little folds between the stitches when cloth is gathered. **1-5** *verb,* **6** *noun.*

gen·e·ra·tion (jen/ə rā/shən), **1** the people born in the same period. Your parents and their friends belong to one generation; you and your friends belong to the next generation. **2** about thirty years, or the time from the birth of one generation to the birth of the next generation. **3** one step in the descent of a family: *The picture showed four generations—great-grandmother, grandmother, mother, and baby.* **4** the act or process of producing: *Steam and water power are used for the generation of electricity. noun.*

grad·u·a·tion (graj/ü ā/shən), **1** a graduating from a school or college. **2** the ceremony of graduating; graduating exercises. *noun.*

ACKNOWLEDGMENTS

Text

Page 6: From *No One Is Going to Nashville* by Mavis Jukes, illustrated by Lloyd Bloom. Text copyright © 1983 by Mavis Jukes. Illustrations copyright © 1983 by Lloyd Bloom. Reprinted by permission of Alfred A. Knopf, Inc.

Page 34: "The Dog That Wouldn't Go Home," by Mavis Jukes. Copyright © by Mavis Jukes, 1991.

Page 38: *We Don't Look Like Our Mom and Dad* by Harriet Langsam Sobol. Copyright © 1984 by Harriet Langsam Sobol. Reprinted by permission of Coward-McCann, Inc.

Page 50: "A Day with the Amish" by Linda Egenes from *Cobblestone's* November, 1987 issue: The Amish. Copyright © 1987, Cobblestone Publishing, Inc., Peterborough, NH 03458. Reprinted by permission of the publisher.

Page 58: From *Yagua Days* by Cruz Martel, pictures by Jerry Pinkney. Copyright © 1976 by Cruz Martel. Copyright © 1976 by Jerry Pinkney for pictures. Used by permission of Dial Books for Young Readers, a division of Penguin Books USA Inc.

Page 78: *I'm the Big Sister Now* by Michelle Emmert. Copyright © 1989 by Michelle Emmert. Illustrations copyright © 1989 by Gail Owens. Excerpt reprinted by permission of Albert Whitman & Company.

Page 94: "My Adopted Grandpa" by Amie Wortman. Reprinted with permission from *Stone Soup*, the magazine by children. Copyright © 1987 by the Children's Art Foundation.

Page 100: Abridged excerpts from *Childtimes: A Three-Generation Memoir* by Eloise Greenfield and Lessie Jones Little. Copyright © 1979 by Eloise Greenfield and Lessie Jones Little. Reprinted by permission of HarperCollins Publishers.

Page 110: From *Nathaniel Talking* by Eloise Greenfield, illustrated by Jan Spivey Gilchrist.

Text copyright © 1988 by Eloise Greenfield, illustration copyright © 1988 by Jan Spivey Gilchrist. Reprinted by permission of Writers and Readers Publishing, Inc.

Page 116: "Writing for Children" by Eloise Greenfield. Copyright © by Eloise Greenfield, 1991.

Artists

Illustrations owned and copyrighted by the illustrator.
Randall Enos cover, 1–4, 119–120, 122–123, 124, 128
Lloyd Bloom 6–34
Jerry Pinkney 58–77
Gail Owens 78–92
Britta Arendt 94–99
Jan Spivey Gilchrist 110–115

Photographs

Unless otherwise acknowledged, all photographs are the property of Scott Foresman.
Page 34: Courtesy of Mavis Jukes
Pages 38–48: Patricia Agre
Pages 51, 54–55, 57: Mel Horst Photography
Page 52: John Zielinski
Page 53: Jerry Irwin
Page 93: Courtesy Arlan & Beverly Emmert, photo courtesy Albert Whitman & Company
Pages 100, 104–105, 116: Courtesy Eloise Greenfield
Page 124: Cathy Koehler
Page 125: Food & Agricultural Organization

Glossary

The contents of the glossary have been adapted from *Beginning Dictionary,* Copyright © 1988 Scott, Foresman and Company and *Intermediate Dictionary,* Copyright © 1988 Scott, Foresman and Company.